JEWISH COOKING

Gail Weinshel Katz

WEATHERVANE BOOKS
New York

I sincerely thank my friends and relatives who contributed their favorite recipes to this book. I especially thank my mother, who very generously shared several of her treasured recipes so that they may be enjoyed by many.

contents

introduction

A Jewish home is a sign of hospitality. A visitor in a Jewish home is almost always offered a meal or at least a sumptuous snack. Food is varied, plentiful, and extremely pleasing to the palate.

Aromas coming from the kitchen are enough to cause hunger pains in even the fullest of stomachs. What's cooking? Well, it might be a challah baking in the oven, chicken soup simmering on the stove, or a delicious honey cake waiting to be sampled.

Immigrants of the Jewish faith coming to America brought with them dishes and ways of cooking from all over the world, which accounts for the large variety in types of dishes and, of course, tastes.

There are the traditional foods associated with the various holidays, such as honey cake for Rosh Hashanah, potato latkes for Chanukah, haman taschen for Purim, and sponge cake for Passover, to name just a few. There is also the traditional challah which shows up weekly on the Sabbath dinner table. You will find many recipes for the above-named holidays, including recipes for all the dishes just mentioned.

One need not be Jewish to cook good Jewish food. Contrary to the belief that Jewish cooking is complicated, it need not be. I've kept most of the recipes in this book uncomplicated, so that even the most inexperienced cook should have no trouble following these recipes and being very pleased with the results.

Even though this is not a Kosher cookbook, there are no recipes containing both dairy products and meat. Therefore, this book is suitable for anyone following Kosher dietary laws.

On the following pages there are a variety of recipes in all categories, some of which have been in my family for many years and are all-time favorites, which I'm happy to share with you.

If you are not familiar with Jewish cooking, I hope this book will help you discover a new taste treat. If you are familiar with Jewish cooking, I hope this book will be a valuable addition to your recipe collection.

Enjoy!

appetizers

chopped eggs and onions

This is one of my family's favorites.

10 hard-cooked eggs
1 cup chopped onions
1 teaspoon salt
¼ teaspoon freshly ground black pepper
3 tablespoons chicken fat (more if necessary)

Chop eggs and onions until fine. Mix in salt, pepper, and fat. Chill several hours.

Spread mixture on crackers or arrange on lettuce leaves; serve as appetizer. Makes 8 servings as an appetizer, 12 servings as a spread.

yummy cocktail hot-dog hors d'oeuvres

These taste like a much more complicated recipe.

1 jar currant jelly
1 small jar mustard
4 dozen boiled cocktail hot dogs

Combine jelly and mustard in saucepan. Stir and cook over low heat until well blended and boiling. Simmer 1 minute. Add hot dogs to sauce; transfer to chafing dish. Makes 12 servings.

baked grapefruit

baked grapefruit

This is a nice first course for a brunch.

3 grapefruit
6 teaspoons dry sherry
6 tablespoons brown sugar
Butter
6 maraschino cherries

Cut each grapefruit in half; vandyke edges. Remove centers; loosen sections from skin with grapefruit knife. Place grapefruit halves in baking dish. Sprinkle each with 1 teaspoon sherry and 1 tablespoon brown sugar. Dot with butter. Bake at 350°F (preheated) about 30 minutes or until tops are golden-colored. Place a cherry in center of each half; serve. Makes 6 servings.

miniature puffs

½ cup butter or vegetable shortening
¼ teaspoon salt
1 cup boiling water
1 cup flour
3 eggs

Put butter, salt, and boiling water in top of double boiler. Add flour all at once, stirring constantly. When mixture is completely blended and leaves sides of pot, remove from heat. Let cool 1 minute. Add eggs, one at a time, beating well after each. Blend thoroughly. Drop by teaspoons onto well-greased cookie sheet, about 2 inches apart. Shape mounds with back of spoon until evenly rounded. Bake at 450°F 10 minutes. Turn temperature to 400°F; bake 15 to 20 minutes or until golden brown and puffed. Cut with sharp knife when completely cool.

These can be filled with many fillings, such as egg salad, tuna salad, chicken salad, cream cheese mixed with chopped walnuts or olives, or any number of choices. They can also be used on a sweet tray, filled with any kind of pudding, or ice cream. Makes about 3 dozen.

stuffed-pepper appetizer

1 medium to large red (or green) pepper
3 ounces blue cheese, softened
7 ounces cream cheese, softened
2 ounces butter, softened
Small squares pumpernickel bread
Grapes for garnish
Stuffed olives for garnish
Parsley for garnish

Wash pepper; cut out membranes.

Mix together well cheeses and butter. Fill pepper with cheese mixture; chill several hours.

Slice pepper; serve with pumpernickel bread. Garnish with grapes, olives, and parsley. Makes about 8 slices.

7

delicious cheese puffs

These are absolutely delectable and so simple to make!

6 ounces cheddar cheese
4 tablespoons butter, softened
¾ cup all-purpose flour

Combine all ingredients. Roll into small balls; bake on cookie sheet at 475°F 8 minutes. Makes approximately 25.

chopped liver

The amount of onions and eggs in this recipe can be adjusted to suit your taste. Some people prefer more of an onion taste; others like the onion flavor to be very subtle. Also, beef or calve's liver can be used instead of chicken liver.

2 medium onions, chopped
Chicken fat
1 pound chicken liver, broiled
  until just done

2 hard-boiled eggs
Salt and freshly ground black
  pepper to taste

Sauté onions in fat.

Grind or chop liver and eggs together. Add onions and enough fat to moisten. Add salt and pepper to taste.

Serve liver on crackers or on bed of lettuce as individual appetizers. Makes 6 servings.

gefilte fish

1½ pounds pike
1½ pounds whitefish
3 large onions, 2 sliced
Salt
Freshly ground black pepper
Generous pinch of sugar
4½ cups water
2 tablespoons matzo meal
2 eggs
2 carrots, sliced

Have fish filleted; reserve heads and bones.

Put 2 sliced onions, fish heads and bones, salt, pepper, sugar, and 4 cups water into large pot. Simmer 1½ hours.

Strain broth. Pour into large pot; bring to boil.

While broth is boiling, grind or chop fish and onion. Add ½ cup water, matzo meal, eggs, salt, and pepper; mix thoroughly.

Wet hands with water; make fish balls. Place in boiling fish broth. Add carrot slices. If necessary, add more water so fish balls are covered. Cook over low heat 2 hours.

If desired, chill fish broth to jell and serve with fish. Place carrot slice on top of each fish ball. Makes 16 to 20 pieces.

chopped herring I

1-pound jar herring tidbits in wine sauce
Juice of 1 lemon
1 tablespoon sugar
1 stale hard roll
2 hard-boiled eggs

Strain herring; make sure all liquid is gone.
Combine lemon juice and sugar; pour over hard roll.
Combine all ingredients in wooden bowl; chop well.
Use herring as an appetizer with crackers. Makes 6 servings.

chopped herring II

1 8-ounce jar marinated herring fillets with onion
1 hard-boiled egg
1 apple, peeled, cored
1 slice white bread, lightly toasted
2 tablespoons sweet red wine

Drain herring. Grind herring, onion, egg, apple, and toast. Add wine; mix thoroughly.
Spread herring on crackers for an appetizer. Makes 6 servings.

herring salad (chopped herring III)

This is delicious on crackers or party rye, or served as an appetizer on a bed of lettuce.

1 large herring, filleted
2 hard-boiled eggs
1 apple, pared
1 medium onion
2 tablespoons vinegar
1 tablespoon oil
Sugar to taste (probably about 2 tablespoons)
3 tablespoons (approximately) fine bread or cracker crumbs
Dash of freshly ground black pepper

Chop herring and eggs until smooth. Grate in apple and onion. Add vinegar and oil. Mix in sugar. Add crumbs and pepper. Mix thoroughly. Refrigerate 1 hour before serving, longer if possible. Makes approximately 3 or 4 servings as an appetizer, about 6 as a spread.

sardine spread

2 cans boneless skinless sardines, drained
2 hard-boiled eggs, chopped fine
½ teaspoon horseradish
1 teaspoon Worcestershire sauce
Salad dressing

Combine all ingredients, using enough salad dressing to moisten to spreading consistency. Spread on party rye for a delicious hors d'oeuvre. Makes 6 servings.

judy's mushroom nosh

These are scrumptious!

nosh pastry

2 cups flour
1 teaspoon salt
¾ cup butter
½ cup sour cream

Mix together flour and salt. Cut in butter. Add sour cream; mix well. Make ball; divide into 3 portions. Roll each portion into thin rectangular piece.

mushroom filling

1 pound fresh mushrooms, cut up
2 medium to large onions, diced
Butter

Salt to taste
Freshly ground black pepper to taste
Garlic powder to taste
Oregano to taste

Sauté mushrooms and onions in butter; add seasonings to taste. Be generous with seasonings, especially pepper, garlic powder, and oregano.

Place filling along edge of dough; roll up jelly-roll fashion. Bake on ungreased baking sheet in 475°F oven 15 minutes or until nicely browned. Check during baking to see if you might need to lower oven to 450°F.

Slice, serve, and enjoy! Makes about 24 to 30 slices.

mighty-good stuffed mushrooms

½ pound large fresh mushrooms
1 egg
Salt
Pepper
Oregano
Matzo meal

Wash mushrooms; remove stems. Put stems in blender with egg, salt, pepper, and oregano. Add matzo meal until of desired thickness. Fill mushroom caps. Place in greased pan; bake at 350°F 15 minutes. Makes approximately 10 to 12, depending on size of mushrooms.

soups and accompaniments

chicken soup

4 quarts water
1 large onion
1 clove garlic, minced
2 teaspoons salt
1 chicken, 5 to 6 pounds,
    whole or cut into pieces
6 carrots, whole or sliced

4 stalks celery with leaves,
    whole or sliced
1 parsnip, whole
1 very ripe tomato
Fresh dill to taste
Fresh parsley to taste

Bring water to boil. Add onion, garlic, and salt. Cover; cook 10 minutes. Add chicken; cook 15 minutes. Add carrots, celery, parsnip, and tomato. Cook slowly, uncovered, until chicken is tender. Add dill and parsley immediately. Remove soup from heat. Cover; let stand. Makes approximately 8 to 10 servings.

clear chicken soup

Thin noodles are very good in this soup.

1 chicken
Cold water
2 carrots
2 celery stalks

1 large onion
Salt to taste
Pepper to taste

Place chicken in large soup pot; cover with cold water. Bring to boil. Skim; add vegetables and seasoning. Boil slowly until chicken is tender. Remove chicken; strain soup. After soup has been chilled you will be able to remove fat. Makes 6 servings.

easy beet borscht

easy beet borscht

1 ¼-inch-thick lemon slice, rind and seeds removed
1 cup diced cooked beets
½ medium onion, chopped

1¾ cups sour cream
¼ teaspoon salt
1 cup crushed ice

Place all ingredients except ice in blender; blend 20 seconds.

Add ice; blend 30 seconds.

Serve borscht in soup cups or small bowls; garnish with dollop of sour cream. Makes about 4 servings.

cabbage soup

2 pounds flanken
4 marrow bones
Salt to taste
1 medium head cabbage, grated

1 large can tomatoes
Salt and pepper to taste
Sugar to taste
Paprika to taste
Boiled potatoes (optional)

Bring meat, bones, and salt to boil in large pot. Skim. Add cabbage, tomatoes, and seasonings. Boil slowly 1½ to 2 hours or until very tender.

Serve soup with boiled potatoes. Makes 4 servings.

delectable pea soup

This soup is delicious!

2 tablespoons butter
1 medium onion, sliced
2 stalks celery, sliced fine
4 carrots, peeled, sliced thin
16 ounces dried green split peas

2½ quarts water
1 teaspoon salt
¼ teaspoon freshly ground black pepper
½ teaspoon garlic powder

Melt butter in large pot. Add onion, celery, and carrots; cook until onion is tender. Add peas, water, salt, pepper, and garlic powder. Simmer, covered, over medium-low heat 1 hour. Makes approximately 6 servings.

spinach borscht

1 quart boiling water
1 pound spinach, washed well, chopped fine
¾ cup sour cream
Salt to taste
Cucumber, cubed
Shallots, diced

Pour boiling water over spinach in large pot; bring to boil again. Remove from heat; cool.

Mix sour cream with salt in large bowl. Add cucumber and shallots. Pour in spinach mixture slowly, stirring constantly until well blended. Chill before serving. Makes 6 to 8 servings.

fresh salmon chowder

2 medium onions, sliced
2 carrots, sliced thin
2 stalks celery with tops, diced
3 potatoes, peeled, cubed
1 cup water
Salt to taste
Freshly ground black pepper to taste
1½ pounds fresh salmon
1 cup milk

Cook onions, carrots, celery, and potatoes 10 minutes in water seasoned with salt and pepper. Place fish and milk in pot. Cook slowly approximately 20 minutes or until fish is done. Makes approximately 4 servings.

egg drops for soup

These are excellent in vegetable soup.

2 eggs
3 tablespoons cold water
½ teaspoon salt
Flour

Combine eggs, water, and salt; beat with fork. Add flour gradually, blending in with fork, until quite thick. More flour will give you a heavier egg drop; less flour means a lighter egg drop. Stir until smooth. Drop from tip of spoon into boiling soup. Simmer 15 minutes. Makes approximately 2 dozen.

passover farfel for soup

This is especially good in chicken soup.

2 cups matzo farfel
3 eggs
½ teaspoon salt

Spread farfel on cookie sheet; heat in moderate oven until browned. Stir occasionally to prevent scorching; cool.

Beat eggs with salt. Add farfel; mix until evenly coated. Place again on cookie sheet; return to oven to dry. When ready, farfel will be separate pieces. Makes approximately 4 servings.

matzo balls II

matzo balls I

2 eggs
2 tablespoons chicken soup
2 tablespoons melted chicken fat
1 teaspoon salt
½ cup matzo meal

Beat eggs. Add soup, fat, and salt; beat again. Fold in matzo meal. Refrigerate about 3 hours.

Shape into balls; drop into pot of boiling, salted water. Cover; boil 20 minutes. Take from water; place in soup. Makes approximately 6 matzo balls.

matzo balls II

4 eggs, separated
2 tablespoons cold water
1 cup matzo meal
½ teaspoon salt

Beat egg yolks with cold water. Fold in stiffly beaten egg whites. Sprinkle in matzo meal and salt. Let mixture stand 10 minutes. Shape into balls; drop into pot of boiling, salted water. Boil 5 minutes, then transfer matzo balls to boiling soup. Simmer 15 minutes. Makes about 12 matzo balls.

kreplach

kreplach dough

1 egg
Pinch of salt
Dash of pepper
¾ cup (approximately) flour

meat filling

1 cup cooked meat
1 onion, chopped fine, sautéed
1 egg
Pinch of salt
Dash of freshly ground black pepper

Beat together 1 egg, salt, and pepper. Gradually beat in enough flour to form stiff dough. Knead well; roll out very thin. Let dough dry about 1 hour. Cut into 3-inch squares.

Mix together filling ingredients.

Place spoonful of meat mixture in center of each dough square. Dampen edges; fold over to form triangle. Let kreplach dry again about 30 minutes. Drop into boiling, salted water; simmer slowly 20 minutes. Or drop right into soup. These are also delicious browned in the oven and served as a side dish, or browned in a skillet. Makes about 16 to 20 kreplach.

15

breakfast and brunch dishes

paul's lox, eggs, and onions

Even though my husband did not create this dish, I felt I had to add his name to the title as it is one of his favorites!

⅛ pound lox (more if desired), cut into small pieces
1 small onion, diced
Butter
4 eggs, beaten
Bagels

Sauté lox and onion in butter until onion is soft. Add eggs; either scramble or let set "omelet style." Serve immediately with bagels for a great breakfast treat. Makes 2 servings.

breakfast puffs

⅓ cup soft shortening
½ cup sugar
1 egg
1½ cups all-purpose flour
1½ teaspoons baking powder
½ teaspoon salt
¼ teaspoon nutmeg
½ cup milk
6 tablespoons melted butter
½ cup sugar and 1 teaspoon cinnamon mixed together

Thoroughly mix together shortening, sugar, and egg.

Sift together dry ingredients. Add to shortening mixture alternately with milk. Fill greased muffin cups two-thirds full. Bake at 350°F 20 minutes or until golden brown. Immediately roll in melted butter, then in sugar and cinnamon mixture. Makes about 12 regular-size or 30 miniature-size muffins.

matzoh brei (fried matzoh)

1 box matzohs
Boiling water
4 or 5 eggs, beaten
Salt to taste
Freshly ground black pepper to taste
Butter or oil for frying

Break matzohs into pieces in large bowl. Add enough boiling water to moisten. There should not be an excess of water; it should all be absorbed by matzohs. Add beaten eggs; it should be quite ''eggy.'' Add salt and pepper; mix well.

Heat butter in skillet. If using oil, use just enough to cover bottom of skillet. Cook on medium-high heat 3 or 4 minutes, turning frequently, only until matzoh is no longer wet. (Some people prefer matzoh crispy and very dry. For this, cook another 2 or 3 minutes.) Serve immediately with your favorite jam. Makes approximately 4 servings.

cheese soufflé omelet

6 tablespoons butter
1 cup finely grated sharp cheddar cheese
1 cup whipping cream
⅛ teaspoon salt
Dash of white pepper
5 eggs, separated
5 tablespoons cold water
Salt to taste
Pepper to taste
Toasted bagels and butter

Heat 4 tablespoons butter in top of double boiler over hot water until bubbly. Add cheese; stir until smooth. Pour in cream very slowly, stirring constantly until smooth and creamy. Stir in ⅛ teaspoon salt and dash of white pepper; keep warm.

Beat egg yolks and water with fork in small bowl until blended. Season with salt and pepper to taste.

Beat egg whites in large bowl until very stiff. Fold egg-yolk mixture into egg whites until mixture is pale-yellow foam.

Heat 2 tablespoons butter in preheated 9-inch omelet pan until butter just begins to brown. Pour egg mixture into pan; cook slowly, pulling edge away from side of pan and leveling top to side with spatula. Pierce through omelet occasionally with tip of spatula to allow heat to rise through omelet. Cook until base is light golden brown and set but top is still foamy. Place in preheated broiler about 3 minutes, until top is lightly browned. Invert onto heated platter. Pour cheese sauce over omelet. Return to broiler; broil just until sauce is browned. Serve immediately with toasted bagels and butter. Makes 2 to 3 servings.

smoked-salmon roll-ups

This is a nice luncheon dish.

20 slices smoked salmon
20 canned asparagus spears, drained
½ cup mayonnaise
Lemon wedges
Parsley

Wrap salmon slices around asparagus spears. Arrange on serving platter. Pipe mayonnaise over roll-ups. Garnish with lemon wedges and parsley. Serve well chilled. Makes 5 or 6 servings.

cheese soufflé omelet

smoked-salmon roll-ups

main dishes

tasty brisket

Brisket is very good made this way. It's even better made up a day or two in advance.

2 cloves garlic, crushed
Salt
Pepper
Paprika
1 brisket, 3 to 4 pounds
2 medium onions, diced
1 large can tomatoes

Make paste of garlic, salt, pepper, and paprika. Be generous with seasonings. Rub mixture over entire brisket. Roast uncovered at 325°F until browned on both sides. Add onions and tomatoes; roast until brisket is tender. Makes approximately 6 servings.

passover brisket

1 brisket, 4 to 5 pounds
Potato starch
Salt to taste
Freshly ground black pepper to taste

3 tomatoes, sliced
2 onions, diced
1 green pepper, diced
½ cup water

Place brisket in roaster; sear on top of stove until brown on all sides. Sprinkle with potato starch, salt, and pepper. Arrange sliced tomatoes on top of brisket; place onions and green pepper in roaster. Add water; roast at 350°F, uncovered, until meat is tender. Makes about 6 servings.

pineapple-glazed brisket

1 brisket, 4 to 5 pounds
Salt to taste
Freshly ground black pepper to taste
1 onion, sliced
2½ cups water

pineapple glaze

1 small can sliced pineapple, drained; reserve juice
6 tablespoons honey
¼ cup pineapple juice
3 tablespoons sugar
½ cup water

Season meat with salt and pepper. Place in Dutch oven with onion and 2½ cups water. Cook slowly until meat is tender, about 2 to 3 hours. Transfer to roasting pan. Place pineapple slices on top of meat; secure with toothpicks.

Combine honey, pineapple juice, sugar, and ½ cup water in saucepan. Bring to boil; simmer 1 minute. Pour over meat. Place in 400°F oven. Roast 30 minutes, basting frequently. You may need to add more water. Makes approximately 5 to 6 servings.

pot roast

3 onions, sliced
2 cloves garlic, crushed
Freshly ground black pepper
Salt
Paprika
1 brisket, 4 to 5 pounds, or top of rib
8 ounces tomato sauce

Place onions in large pot. Add small amount of water; simmer 5 minutes.

Make paste of garlic, pepper, salt, and paprika. Rub on meat. Cook meat until lightly browned on all sides. Add small amount of water. Cover; simmer on low heat 45 minutes. Add tomato sauce. Cook, covered, 3 hours or until meat is tender. Let cool before slicing. Makes 5 to 6 servings.

brisket with sauerkraut

4 cups sauerkraut, fresh or canned
1 brisket, 4 or 5 pounds
2 potatoes, grated
1 tablespoon sugar
1 teaspoon caraway seeds
1 whole large onion
Boiling water

Place half of sauerkraut in Dutch oven; place meat on top.

Mix together potatoes, sugar, caraway seeds, and remaining sauerkraut. Put mixture on top of brisket. Add onion and boiling water to cover. Simmer, covered, on low heat about 3 hours or until meat is tender. Makes 4 to 6 servings.

baked stuffed peppers

4 medium green peppers
4 medium red peppers
Boiling salted water
1 pound ground beef
1 cup chopped onion
2 tablespoons margarine or oil
2 10½-ounce cans condensed
tomato soup

4 cups cooked rice
2 teaspoons Worcestershire
sauce
1 teaspoon salt
Freshly ground black pepper
to taste

Remove tops and seeds from peppers. Cook in boiling, salted water about 5 minutes; drain well.

In large skillet brown beef and onion in margarine. Stir in 1 can soup, rice, Worcestershire sauce, salt, and pepper. Remove from heat; mix thoroughly. Spoon meat mixture into peppers. Place in baking dish; bake in 375°F oven 30 minutes. Heat remaining can of soup; serve over peppers. Makes 8 servings.

baked stuffed peppers

bird's tsimmes

This recipe was contributed by the mother of a friend of mine, whose nickname is "Bird." This recipe has apparently been in the family for many years and is a family favorite.

1 piece of chuck or brisket, whichever you prefer	Brown sugar
Carrots, sliced	Potato-kugel mixture
Sweet potatoes, sliced or cut into chunks	

Place meat in roaster. Put carrots and sweet potatoes around roast. Sprinkle with brown sugar.

Mix up potato kugel; pour over meat and vegetables in roaster. Cover; roast in 350°F oven until meat and vegetables are tender. Uncover for last 15 minutes.

meat tzimmes

1 pound chuck meat, cubed	Water
3 pounds carrots, peeled, sliced	1 cup honey
	Dash of salt
2 large sweet potatoes, peeled, sliced	½ cup sugar

Place meat, carrots, and sweet potatoes in very large pot filled three-fourths of way with water. Add honey, salt, and sugar. Cook on low heat 2 hours. Makes 4 servings.

yummy brisket

1 package onion soup mix	Freshly ground black pepper to taste
2 cloves garlic, crushed	1 3- to 4-pound brisket
4 ounces dry red wine	
Salt to taste (use sparingly)	

Mix together soup mix, garlic, wine, salt, and pepper. Marinate brisket in mixture overnight; turn occasionally.

Place brisket in roasting pan. Pour sauce over; cover tightly with aluminum foil. Bake at 375°F 2½ hours or until tender. Makes 6 servings.

baked steak

4 tablespoons margarine, cut into small pieces	2 large onions, sliced
1 large steak, 2 to 3 inches thick, cut of your choice	1 medium green pepper, sliced
	1 bottle chili sauce

Dot bottom of baking pan with half of margarine. Place steak on top of margarine; top with rest of margarine. Cover steak with onions, green pepper, and chili sauce. Bake in preheated 450°F oven 1 hour. Test for desired doneness. Bake few minutes longer, if necessary. Makes 2 servings.

ground-beef casserole

1 pound ground beef
1 medium onion, diced
Salt, pepper, and garlic
  powder to taste

8 ounces cooked elbow
  macaroni
1 small can tomato sauce

Brown ground beef and onion in large skillet. Add seasonings, macaroni, and tomato sauce. Mix thoroughly; transfer to casserole. Place in 325°F oven; bake 20 minutes. Makes 4 to 5 servings.

ground-beef – potato pie

This is delicious, and children like it.

3 medium potatoes, cooked
1 egg
1 onion, diced, fried in small
  amount of oil
1 pound ground beef

Salt to taste
Freshly ground black pepper
  to taste
Garlic powder to taste
Paprika

Mash potatoes with egg and onion. Spread half of mixture in greased casserole dish. Spread meat seasoned with salt, pepper, and garlic powder on top. Cover with remaining potatoes; sprinkle with paprika. Bake in preheated 350°F oven 1 hour. Makes 4 servings.

hamburger roll-up

This is very tasty!

meat mixture

1 large onion, diced
2 stalks celery, diced
1 small green pepper, diced
Oil for frying

1¼ pounds ground beef
Salt to taste
Freshly ground black pepper
  to taste

Sauté onion, celery, and green pepper in oil until soft but not yet brown. Add meat; sauté until brown. Add salt and pepper. Remove from heat; cool.

dough

1¾ cups flour
4 teaspoons baking powder
½ teaspoon salt
5 tablespoons margarine
⅔ cup water
Mustard

Mix together flour, baking powder, and salt. Cut margarine into mixture until consistency of coarse meal. Add water, few drops at a time, mashing with fork until well mixed. Roll out dough on floured board into rectangle; spread with mustard.

Spread meat mixture on dough. Roll up as for jelly roll. Place on ungreased pan, seam-side-down. Make few vents in top to allow steam to escape. Bake at 375°F until brown, about 45 minutes. Cool slightly before slicing. Makes 4 servings.

24

easy lasagna

Garlic powder to taste
Onion powder to taste
Salt to taste
Freshly ground black pepper
   to taste
Pinch of oregano
1 pound ground beef
½ box (8 ounces) lasagna
   noodles
1 large can tomato sauce

Add seasonings to ground beef. Brown meat in skillet.

Boil noodles; cut each noodle in half the short way. Place 2 or 3 tablespoons meat mixture on each noodle; roll up. Place seam-side-down in pan; pour tomato sauce over. Bake at 350°F 30 to 40 minutes. Makes 4 servings.

meat loaf

1½ pounds ground beef
1 onion, chopped
¾ cup quick-cooking oats
Salt to taste
Freshly ground black pepper
   to taste
1 egg, beaten
1 cup tomato juice

Mix together all ingredients. Place into loaf pan. Bake in preheated 350°F oven 1 hour. Makes 4 servings.

filled meat loaf

1 medium potato, grated
1 large onion, grated
1½ pounds ground beef
Salt to taste
Freshly ground black pepper
   to taste
½ cup water
4 hard-boiled eggs, peeled,
   left whole

Add potato and onion to beef. Add salt, pepper, and water; mix well.

Heat well-greased loaf pan. Place half of meat mixture in pan, pressing meat firmly in pan. Place eggs in row along center of meat. Cover with balance of meat. Bake in 350°F oven 1 hour and 15 minutes. Makes 4 servings.

beef porcupine balls

1 pound ground beef
½ cup uncooked rice
¼ cup chopped onion
Salt to taste
Freshly ground black pepper
   to taste
2 tablespoons oil
2 small cans tomato sauce
1 tablespoon sugar
2 tomato-sauce cans water

Mix together beef, rice, onion, salt, and pepper. Form into small balls. Fry in oil until brown. Drain off as much oil as possible. Add tomato sauce, sugar, and water. Cover; simmer 45 minutes. Makes 4 servings.

breaded lamb chops

4 shoulder lamb chops
2 cups fine cracker crumbs

2 eggs, beaten
Oil for frying

Pat lamb chops dry. Dip in crumbs, then into beaten eggs and back into crumbs. Fry in heated oil in skillet until browned on both sides, turning once. Makes 4 servings.

casserole of lamb chops

This is very, very good and is a one-dish meal.

4 shoulder lamb chops
Flour
Fat for browning chops
4 medium potatoes, cubed
2 cups sliced carrots
1 cup frozen peas

1 small onion, diced
Salt to taste
Freshly ground black pepper
  to taste
¼ cup hot water
3 tablespoons minced parsley

Trim fat from chops. Dip in flour; brown in hot fat.

Place potatoes, carrots, peas, and onion in large casserole. Sprinkle with salt and pepper. Pour hot water over vegetables. Place chops on top; sprinkle with parsley and a little more salt and pepper. Cover tightly; bake in 350°F oven 1 hour. Makes 4 servings.

lamb stew

3 pounds lamb, cut up
3 tablespoons hot melted
  Schmaltz (see Index)
2 large onions, diced
1 large carrot, diced
1 parsnip, diced
1 white turnip, diced
1 cup small pieces green beans

1 pound potatoes, peeled,
  cubed
1 cup thinly sliced celery,
  including leaves
1 tablespoon minced parsley
1 clove garlic, minced
1 teaspoon salt
¼ teaspoon paprika

Braise meat in schmaltz. Add diced onions; cook until lightly browned. Add remaining ingredients. Cover; cook slowly about 1 hour and 15 minutes. Stir gently 2 or 3 times during cooking. Makes 4 servings.

breaded veal cutlets

Freshly ground black pepper
Oil for frying
3 veal cutlets

2 eggs, beaten
1 cup matzo meal
Salt

Beat eggs in bowl.

Mix together matzo meal, salt, and pepper on plate.

Heat oil in frying pan.

Dip cutlets into eggs on both sides, then into matzo-meal mixture. Fry over low heat about 15 minutes on each side, until golden brown. Makes 3 servings.

apricot chicken

1 3-pound chicken, cut up
3 tablespoons apricot jam
  (chunky is good)
1 tablespoon lemon juice
1 tablespoon mayonnaise
1 tablespoon catsup
1 package onion soup mix

Place chicken skin-side-up in roasting pan.

Mix other ingredients together in saucepan; bring to boil, stirring constantly. Remove from heat; pour over chicken. Bake uncovered at 350°F 1½ hours or until chicken is tender. Makes 4 servings.

festive chicken

This recipe requires a little extra work and time but is well worth it. It is unusual and unusually good!

1 3-pound chicken, quartered
3 tablespoons oil
1 large onion, sliced
1 large can tomatoes
1 green pepper, diced
1 small can button
  mushrooms, drained
2 scallions, diced
1 large can pineapple chunks,
  drained; reserve liquid

Brown chicken in hot oil.

Place sliced onions in roaster. Add chicken, tomatoes, pepper, mushrooms, scallions, and pineapple chunks. Bake at 350°F 30 minutes.

pineapple sauce

8 ounces pineapple juice
½ cup vinegar
½ cup sugar
1 tablespoon flour

Stir together 6 ounces pineapple juice, vinegar, and sugar in saucepan. Place over low heat.

Make paste of flour and 2 ounces pineapple juice. Add all at once to hot mixture, stirring briskly. Cook, stirring constantly, until thickened.

Pour sauce over chicken and vegetables in roaster. Bake 1 hour. Makes approximately 4 servings.

chicken and noodles

1 chicken, 5 to 6 pounds, from
  soup
5 tablespoons Schmaltz (see
  Index)
1 large onion, diced
4 cups cooked noodles,
  medium or wide, drained
Paprika

Remove fat and skin from chicken.

Melt schmaltz in large skillet; brown onion. Add noodles, mixing with onions 3 minutes. Add chicken; mix well. Transfer to baking dish. Sprinkle top with paprika. Cover; bake at 375°F 25 minutes. Uncover; place under broiler 2 minutes or until top is browned. Makes 4 to 6 servings.

easy and tasty roasted chicken

1 roasting chicken, about 5 pounds
2 tablespoons margarine
Freshly ground black pepper
Paprika
1 garlic clove, cut into very fine pieces
2 onions, cut into quarters

Prepare chicken for roasting. Dot with margarine. Sprinkle with pepper, paprika, and garlic. Place onions around chicken in pan. Roast in 350°F oven until tender and nicely browned on top. If desired, add potatoes or vegetables while chicken is roasting. Baste chicken occasionally while roasting. Makes 4 to 6 servings.

baked fish in milk

1 pound fish fillets, your choice
Flour
½ teaspoon salt
Dash of pepper
1½ cups milk

Wash fillets; pat dry. Place in greased baking dish. Dust with flour; sprinkle with salt and pepper. Pour milk over fish. Bake at 375°F about 30 minutes or until fish is tender. Makes 3 or 4 servings.

kasha-stuffed fish fillets

6 fish fillets (sole or flounder)
Salt to taste
Freshly ground black pepper
  to taste
8 ounces kasha
1 pint salted water

1 medium to large onion,
  chopped
4 tablespoons butter
1 medium onion, sliced
1 cup milk
2 tablespoons butter

Wash fish; pat dry. Sprinkle with salt and pepper.

Boil kasha in salted water until water is absorbed.

Fry chopped onion in butter; add to kasha. Place spoonful of kasha mixture on each fillet of fish. Roll up; secure with toothpicks

Grease baking dish; arrange sliced onions on bottom. Place fish fillets on onions. Add milk; dot with butter. Bake at 350°F 30 minutes. Makes 6 servings.

pickled fish

3 pounds whitefish, cut into
  2-inch slices (use head also)
3 cups water
1 teaspoon salt
1 medium onion, sliced

½ cup white vinegar
¼ cup sugar
1 tablespoon pickling spices
1 medium onion, sliced

Place fish in large pot. Add water, salt, and 1 onion. Bring to boil; simmer 15 minutes. Discard fish head. Remove fish; place in bowl. Measure 2½ cups broth. Add vinegar, sugar, pickling spices, and 1 onion. Bring to a boil; cook 5 minutes. Pour over fish. Chill 24 hours (at least) before serving. Makes approximately 8 servings.

side dishes

sandie's matzo farfel ring

This is so good you'll want to make it all year, not only for Passover!

1 cup minced onions
1 cup diced celery
¼ cup chicken fat or oil
2 eggs, slightly beaten
1 cup chicken broth,
   homemade or canned

1 teaspoon salt
¼ teaspoon freshly ground
   black pepper
1 teaspoon paprika
1½ cups boiling water
3½ cups matzo farfel

Sauté onions and celery in fat until soft but not brown.

Combine eggs with chicken broth. Add salt, pepper, and paprika. Stir in water.

Add farfel to vegetables. Pour in liquid; allow to stand until liquids are absorbed (about 10 minutes). Turn into greased ring mold. Bake at 350°F 30 minutes.

Turn out ring onto hot platter. Fill center with vegetables in sauce or with diced turkey or chicken in gravy. Makes 6 servings.

mother's mock kishka

This is delicious!

2 boxes Tam Tam crackers
3 medium carrots
2 stalks celery
1 large Spanish onion
2 eggs, well beaten
½ teaspoon salt
½ cup oil

Grind together crackers, carrots, celery, and onion. Add eggs, salt, and oil; mix well. Make 3 or 4 long rolls; wrap in aluminum foil. Bake at 350°F 30 minutes. Open foil; bake 15 minutes. (These can be frozen before baking.)

Cut into small slices and serve as appetizer, or cut into larger slices and serve as accompaniment to an entree. Makes approximately 3 dozen as an appetizer, 4 servings as an entree accompaniment.

meat kreplach

These are very simple to make and quite good.

kreplach dough

1 cup flour
1 egg
Pinch of salt

Mix ingredients. Knead well; roll out on floured board. Cut into circles or squares.

meat filling

1 cup cooked chicken or leftover meat
Grated onion
Salt to taste
Pepper to taste

Grind chicken with onion. Add salt and pepper; mix well.

Put 1 tablespoon meat mixture on each dough circle. Shape into triangles. Fry in hot oil in skillet until browned. Makes approximately 12 kreplach.

potato kugel I

1 pound freshly boiled potatoes
Salt to taste
Freshly ground black pepper to taste
3 tablespoons chicken fat
2 eggs, separated

Mash potatoes very well with salt, pepper, fat, and egg yolks.

Beat egg whites until very stiff. Pour into potato mixture. Pour mixture into greased baking dish. Bake at 400 to 425°F 30 minutes or until browned on top. Makes 4 servings.

potato kugel II

6 medium potatoes, grated
1 large onion, grated
2 eggs, well beaten
1 teaspoon salt
½ cup melted chicken fat or
   butter
2 tablespoons flour
2 tablespoons chicken fat or butter

Mix together potatoes and onion; drain off liquid. Add eggs, salt, ½ cup fat, and flour; mix well.

Melt 2 tablespoons fat or butter in baking dish. Pour potato mixture into baking dish. Bake in preheated 375°F oven approximately 1 hour or until browned. (You may need to start kugel at 400°F, then turn oven down to 375 or 350°F.) Makes about 12 servings.

sweet kugel

4 tablespoons apricot preserves
2 eggs, beaten
2 apples, peeled, sliced
3 tablespoons sugar
Juice of ¼ lemon
¼ cup raisins
8 ounces narrow noodles, cooked
⅛ cup oil
Cinnamon

Add preserves, eggs, apples, sugar, lemon juice, and raisins to noodles.

Heat oil in 7 × 11-inch baking dish. Add noodle mixture. Sprinkle cinnamon on top. Bake in preheated 350°F oven 1 hour. Makes approximately 10 servings.

cheese latkes

1 pound cottage cheese
3 eggs
3 tablespoons milk
½ cup flour
Salt to taste
Pepper to taste
Oil for frying

Mix all ingredients together.

Heat oil in skillet. Drop mixture by tablespoonfuls into hot skillet; fry until golden brown. Turn once to brown on both sides. Makes about 12 pancakes.

matzo-meal pancakes

½ cup matzo meal
½ teaspoon salt
½ cup water
2 egg yolks
2 egg whites, well beaten

Mix matzo meal, salt, water, and egg yolks in large bowl. Fold in egg whites. Drop from spoon into hot skillet, using butter or vegetable shortening. Makes approximately 16 medium pancakes.

noodle pancakes

This is a good side dish. It is also good for using leftover noodles.

8 ounces egg noodles, broad or fine
3 quarts boiling, salted water
2 eggs
Pinch of salt
¼ cup butter or margarine, melted
Butter or margarine for frying pancakes

Cook noodles in boiling, salted water until tender. Drain; rinse in colander. Drain well.

In large mixing bowl beat eggs with salt. Add melted butter and noodles; toss until well mixed.

Melt butter in skillet. Drop spoonfuls of noodle mixture; brown on both sides. Makes 4 to 6 servings.

potato pancakes

This recipe makes crisp pancakes. Great with applesauce or sour cream.

6 large potatoes
2 medium onions
6 eggs, well beaten
4 tablespoons flour
2 teaspoons salt

Grate potatoes and onions. Add beaten eggs to mixture. Add flour and salt; mix well. Fry in deep fat in frying pan, dropping from tablespoon. Turn only once; drain on paper toweling. Makes about 3 dozen pancakes.

blender potato pancakes

2 eggs
2 large potatoes, cubed (do not peel)
1 medium onion, diced
Salt to taste
Freshly ground black pepper to taste
2 tablespoons flour
Vegetable oil for frying

Put eggs in blender; add potatoes and onion a little at a time. Blend about 15 seconds; repeat. At last addition add salt, pepper, and flour. Drop by tablespoonfuls into ¼-inch hot oil. Turn once to brown on both sides. Drain on paper toweling.

Serve pancakes with sour cream or applesauce. Makes approximately 15 pancakes.

mother's passover apple fritters

Very, very good!

1 cup matzoh meal
3 eggs
2 tablespoons oil
½ teaspoon salt
½ cup water
3 medium tart apples, peeled, cut into small pieces
Oil for deep frying
Sugar and cinnamon

Mix together matzoh meal, eggs, 2 tablespoons oil, salt, and water. Add apples; blend well. Drop by spoonfuls into deep hot oil; fry until golden brown. Lift out with slotted spoon; drain on paper toweling. Sprinkle with sugar and cinnamon. Serve hot or cold. Makes approximately 4 servings as an addition to a meal.

noodle pudding

16 ounces medium noodles
Pinch of salt
8 eggs, separated
½ cup sugar
½ cup orange juice
2 tablespoons lemon juice
¾ cup crushed cornflakes
2 ounces raisins

Boil noodles 10 minutes with pinch of salt; drain. Rinse with cold water; drain again.

Beat egg whites with pinch of salt until peaks are formed. Add sugar; beat 30 seconds. Add yolks; beat 1 minute. Add orange juice and lemon juice. Gradually add cornflakes and raisins. Add noodles; mix thoroughly.

Grease 9 × 13-inch pan with oil. Heat pan in oven. Place noodle mixture in pan. Bake at 350°F 45 minutes. Makes 8 servings.

mother's passover apple fritters

vegetable dishes

rice-stuffed cabbage rolls

1 head cabbage
1 cup long-grain rice
3 cups boiling salted water
1 tablespoon butter
1 tablespoon paprika
¼ cup currants
2 tablespoons finely chopped parsley
Melted butter

Place cabbage in steamer; steam 1½ hours or until tender.

Cook rice in water about 20 minutes or until tender; drain.

Combine rice, 1 tablespoon butter, paprika, currants, and parsley. Stir until butter is melted.

Remove cabbage from steamer; plunge into cold water to loosen leaves. Cut out any hard core; separate leaves. Place about 1 tablespoon rice mixture on each leaf. Overlap sides; roll up.

Place rolls on serving platter. Pour melted butter over rolls. Serve immediately. Makes 6 to 8 servings.

rice-stuffed cabbage rolls

broccoli casserole

brussels sprouts with cheese—noodle ring

38

creamed beets

1 tablespoon lemon juice
½ teaspoon salt
3 cups cooked, mashed beets
½ cup sour cream
½ cup crumbs
1 tablespoon butter

Add lemon juice and salt to beets. Fold in sour cream. Top with crumbs; dot with butter. Brown under broiler. Makes approximately 4 servings.

broccoli casserole

1 package frozen broccoli
Small amount boiling water
1¼ cups milk
3 eggs, lightly beaten
½ teaspoon salt
½ teaspoon nutmeg
½ cup grated cheese

Preheat oven to 350°F.

Cook broccoli in boiling water 3 minutes; drain well. Pour milk into small saucepan; bring to boil. Cool to lukewarm.

Mix eggs with salt and nutmeg. Add milk and cheese, beating constantly. Pour into greased baking dish. Add broccoli. Bake about 35 minutes or until knife inserted in center comes out clean. Serve hot. Makes 4 servings.

brussels sprouts with cheese–noodle ring

4 cups fresh brussels sprouts
1¼ teaspoons salt
3 tablespoons butter
⅛ teaspoon freshly ground black pepper

Wash and trim brussels sprouts. Place in saucepan with 1 inch boiling water and salt. Bring to boil; cook 5 minutes. Cover; reduce heat. Simmer 15 minutes or until brussels sprouts are crisp-tender; drain. Add butter and pepper; toss lightly until butter is melted. Spoon most of brussels sprouts into center of Cheese-Noodle Ring; place remaining brussels sprouts around ring. Makes 6 servings.

cheese–noodle ring

1 pound wide noodles
3 tablespoons butter
2 cups grated cheddar cheese
2 teaspoons Worcestershire sauce

Cook noodles in boiling, salted water until tender; drain. Add butter; toss until butter is melted. Pour into well-greased ring mold; place mold in pan of hot water. Bake in preheated 350°F oven 25 minutes. Unmold onto serving plate.

Melt cheese in double boiler; stir in Worcestershire sauce. Pour over noodle ring.

mother's carrot ring

Absolutely scrumptious! My family is always happy to see me bring this to the table.

1 cup vegetable shortening	Pinch of salt
½ cup brown sugar	1 cup grated carrots
1¼ cups flour	1 tablespoon water
1 teaspoon baking soda	1 tablespoon lemon juice
1 teaspoon baking powder	1 egg

Cream shortening and sugar. Add dry ingredients; mix well. Add rest of ingredients; mix until well blended. Bake in greased ring mold, covered loosely with foil, at 325°F 1 hour. Makes just enough for my family of 4!

carrot tzimmes I

1 tablespoon chicken fat	8 ounces water
1 pound carrots, peeled, coarsely grated	2 sweet potatoes, peeled, cut into small pieces
1 tablespoon sugar	1 tablespoon flour
Dash of salt	

Melt fat in saucepan. Add carrots, sugar, and salt. Cook very slowly ½ hour. Add water. Cook 20 minutes. Add sweet potatoes; sprinkle flour over all. Cook ½ hour. Makes 5 to 6 servings.

carrot tzimmes II

4 tablespoons margarine	¼ teaspoon salt
1 pound carrots, peeled, sliced	½ cup flour
½ cup brown sugar	4 tablespoons cold water
1 cup water	

Melt margarine in pan; cook carrots until lightly browned. Add sugar, water, and salt. Cover; cook until carrots are tender.

Mix flour and water thoroughly; add to carrots. Heat 3 minutes, stirring constantly. Makes 4 servings.

easy but excellent cauliflower

1 head cauliflower	¼ cup bread crumbs
Small amount of water	2 teaspoons parsley
1 teaspoon salt	Salt
3 tablespoons butter or margarine	Pepper
	Garlic powder

Cook cauliflower in water with 1 teaspoon salt over medium heat until soft. Drain well. Before cauliflower cools, coat with butter, bread crumbs, parsley, and seasonings. Cover pot; let sit until butter or margarine has melted. Serve immediately. Makes 4 to 5 servings.

eggplant casserole

This is a delicious treat for eggplant lovers.

2 medium eggplants
½ cup flour
Oil for frying
2 medium onions, chopped
  fine
1 8-ounce can tomato sauce

¼ cup cornflake crumbs
Salt to taste
Powdered ginger to taste
2 tablespoons butter
Bread or cornflake crumbs

Slice unpared eggplants into ¼-inch slices. Dip in flour. Fry in oil until browned on both sides. Drain on paper toweling.

Chop eggplant in large bowl. Add onions, tomato sauce, ¼ cup cornflake crumbs, salt, and ginger; mix well. Place in baking dish; dot with butter. Sprinkle top with small amount of crumbs. Bake at 350°F 20 minutes or until browned. Makes 4 to 5 servings.

creamed spinach

1 pound spinach, cleaned,
  chopped fine

½ cup heavy cream, whipped
Pinch of salt

Cook spinach 2 minutes in covered pot, without adding water. Cool. Fold in cream; add salt. Makes 4 servings.

candied
sweet potatoes

1 tablespoon shortening
1 cup brown sugar
1 cup orange juice
Pinch of salt

6 sweet potatoes, uncooked,
  peeled, cut in half
  lengthwise

Melt shortening in large skillet. Add sugar, juice, and salt; mix together. Bring to boil. Add potatoes. Simmer, covered, until potatoes are tender, turning and basting frequently. Makes 12 servings.

vegetable casserole

1 16-ounce can asparagus
  spears
1 16-ounce can small peas
1 can cream of mushroom
  soup

American cheese, cut into
  small pieces
Potato chips, crumbled

Make layers in casserole, starting with asparagus, then peas and soup. Place cheese on top, then potato chips. Bake in 350°F oven 25 minutes or until heated through. Makes 4 servings.

41

salads

unusual salad

1 head lettuce, shredded
½ cup chopped green pepper
½ cup thinly sliced celery
½ cup chopped onion
1 package frozen peas,
   cooked, cooled

1 pint Miracle Whip mixed
   with 2 tablespoons sugar
1 cup grated sharp cheddar
   cheese

Place each ingredient in large salad bowl in order given. Cover; refrigerate 24 hours. Makes approximately 10 servings.

winter salad

Segments from 1 large
   grapefruit
Segments from 1 large orange
1 cup shredded lettuce
½ cup mayonnaise

1 tablespoon orange juice
Chopped nuts
Grated orange rind to taste
Maraschino cherries

Arrange grapefruit and orange segments (seeds removed) in alternating rows on bed of shredded lettuce.

Combine ½ cup mayonnaise with 1 tablespoon orange juice. Add chopped nuts and grated orange rind to taste; spoon over salad just before serving. Garnish with maraschino cherries. Makes 2 servings.

strawberry gelatin squares

This is a very pretty and delicious gelatin salad.

2 small or 1 large package red gelatin
2 cups boiling water
1 package frozen strawberries, thawed

1 small can crushed pineapple, drained
1 large ripe banana, diced fine
1 cup sour cream

Dissolve gelatin in boiling water. Add strawberries, pineapple, and banana; mix well. Pour half the mixture into 8-inch-square pan. Chill until firm. Spoon sour cream over gelatin, then pour remaining gelatin over. Chill until firm. Serve on lettuce. Makes 9 squares.

garlic-lover's salad dressing

This is *so* good on green salad!

6 large cloves garlic, crushed
Juice of 2 lemons
1 teaspoon salt
Salad oil

Combine garlic, lemon juice, and salt. Measure; add as much salad oil as mixture. Store in covered jar in refrigerator. Shake and strain before using. Makes enough for about 3 medium salads.

fresh garlic

breads and rolls

mother's onion bread

This bread is unusual and very tasty. It's hard to stop at one slice!

6 large onions, diced
Small amount oil
9 cups flour
1 2-ounce cake of yeast or 3 packages dry yeast
4 cups lukewarm water
6 tablespoons oil
4 teaspoons salt
4 tablespoons sugar
Egg yolk beaten with small amount of cold water

Sauté onions in small amount of oil; set aside.

Put flour into large bowl. Make well in flour; crumble yeast into well. Mix with fork, adding ½ cup water. Let stand in warm place until dough doubles in size. Add oil, salt, sugar, and rest of water. Knead dough; let rise. Knead again; let rise. Cut dough into 6 pieces. Roll each piece into rectangle; spread with some of onions. Roll up. Brush tops with egg yolk beaten with small amount of cold water. Let rise again. Bake on cookie sheets or baking pans at 350°F 45 to 50 minutes. Makes 6 loaves.

challah

challah

2 packages yeast
2½ cups warm water
6 tablespoons sugar
2 teaspoons salt
⅓ cup vegetable oil
4 eggs
8⅔ cups flour
1 egg yolk beaten with 1 teaspoon water
Poppy or sesame seeds (optional)

In large bowl dissolve yeast in warm water. Add sugar, salt, oil, eggs, and 6 cups flour. Beat well with wooden spoon; gradually add more flour until dough is too stiff to beat with spoon. Place remaining flour on board; knead dough until smooth and all flour is absorbed and dough is no longer sticky. Place dough in large covered bowl; let rise in warm place 1½ hours or until doubled. Punch down; divide into 4 parts, shaping each loaf as desired. Place each loaf in well-greased pan; let rise in warm place until doubled (about 1 hour). Brush tops with egg-yolk mixture; sprinkle with seeds if desired. Bake in preheated 375°F oven 25 to 30 minutes or until loaves are golden brown. Cool on racks. Makes 4 loaves.

onion flats

These take very little effort and are very good.

5 ounces butter
2 cups all-purpose flour
1 medium onion, finely grated
⅛ teaspoon salt
Pinch of pepper
1 egg, well beaten
1 egg, beaten, for glaze
Poppy seeds (optional)

Cut butter into flour. Mix in onion, salt, and pepper. Add well-beaten egg; mix well. Knead lightly in bowl. Roll out (experiment with the thickness you prefer); cut into squares. Brush with egg; sprinkle with poppy seeds. Bake on cookie sheet at 400°F 10 to 15 minutes or until lightly browned. Makes approximately 2 to 3 dozen squares, depending on size.

passover popovers

These are a delightful addition to any Passover meal.

1 cup water
¼ cup vegetable shortening or butter
Dash of salt
1 cup matzo meal
3 eggs

Put water, shortening, and salt in saucepan. Bring to boil. Pour in matzo meal; stir well. Remove from heat. Add eggs, one at a time, beating well after each. Spoon onto greased cookie sheet. Bake at 375°F 45 minutes. Makes approximately 12 popovers.

desserts

mandelbroit (mandel bread)

3 eggs
1 cup sugar
½ cup oil
3 cups flour, sifted
3 teaspoons baking powder
¼ teaspoon salt
1½ cups slivered almonds
1 teaspoon almond flavoring
1 teaspoon vanilla
½ teaspoon cinnamon
2 tablespoons orange juice
Grated rind of orange

Beat eggs well. Add sugar gradually. Add other ingredients in order given; blend together well. Form into 5 rolls. Bake on slightly oiled baking pans in 400°F oven 25 minutes. While still hot, cut into slices. Place in pan; put into 350°F oven for few minutes to dry. Makes about 60 slices.

Variations: Omit slivered almonds and add chocolate chips to dough, or add almonds to part of dough, and chocolate chips to part. Your favorite jam can be added to portion of dough also. To do this, make an indentation in roll of dough. Spoon jam in; close up indentation.

easy and delightful banana nut bread

⅓ cup shortening
1 cup sugar
1 cup mashed bananas

1 teaspoon baking soda
2 cups all-purpose flour
1 cup chopped nuts

Cream shortening and sugar. Add bananas, baking soda, and flour; mix well. Add nuts. Bake in greased loaf pan at 350°F 1 hour or until browned on top. Makes approximately 15 slices.

super-easy apple cake

3 medium apples, peeled, cored, cut into cubes
Cinnamon
1½ cups flour
1 cup sugar
1½ teaspoons baking powder

½ teaspoon (scant) salt
½ cup oil
2 eggs
⅛ cup orange juice
1½ teaspoons vanilla

Sprinkle apples generously with cinnamon; let stand while preparing batter.

Place flour, sugar, baking powder, and salt in large bowl. Mix with fork; make well in center. Into well add oil, eggs, orange juice, and vanilla. Mix thoroughly with fork. Fold in apples. Batter will be thick. Pour into greased 8-inch-square baking pan. Bake at 350°F 35 to 40 minutes or until browned. Do not overbake. Toothpick should not be completely dry when cake is tested. Makes about 9 pieces.

janet's perfection cake

This recipe truly produces, as the name implies, a cake of perfection. This is my mother's recipe that dates back many years. Since I can remember, this has been the traditional birthday cake in my family. However, this cake is a bit tricky, only insofar as catching the boiling sugar and water at exactly the right time. This is delicious with a seven-minute frosting and/or ice cream and is also great when split and filled and frosted with chocolate whipped cream.

2 cups sugar
½ cup water
9 jumbo eggs or 10 large eggs, separated
2 teaspoons cream of tartar

Pinch of salt
1 teaspoon vanilla
1½ cups sifted cake flour (sift, then measure)

Put sugar and water into small saucepan; let come to slow boil, stirring occasionally.

Meanwhile beat egg whites until foamy. Add cream of tartar; beat until soft peaks form.

Let sugar and water boil, mixing frequently, until it almost "spins a thread." Slowly pour sugar mixture into egg whites while beating egg whites to peaks again.

Beat egg yolks together with salt and vanilla until well blended and thickening. Fold yolk mixture carefully into egg whites, then fold in flour. Bake in ungreased tube pan at 350°F 1 hour. Cake should be very large and nicely browned on top. Makes about 12 servings.

passover chocolate sponge cake

12 eggs, separated
1½ cups sugar, sifted
2 tablespoons cold water
Juice and rind of 1 orange

2 bars Passover sweet
  chocolate, grated
¾ cup cake meal

Beat egg yolks until light. Add sugar; beat again. Add water, juice, and rind. Add chocolate and cake meal. Fold in stiffly beaten egg whites. Bake in tube pan at 350°F 1 hour. Invert to cool. Makes approximately 12 slices.

sour-cream cake

This cake is very tasty. Nobody will guess it was so easy to make.

¼ pound butter, softened
1 cup sugar
2 eggs
2 cups sifted cake flour
½ pint sour cream
½ teaspoon vanilla
1 teaspoon baking soda
1 teaspoon baking powder

Blend all ingredients together. Pour into greased 8-inch-square pan. Bake at 350°F about 40 minutes. Test for doneness. Makes about 12 pieces.

haman taschen

2 eggs
½ cup sugar
½ cup oil
1 teaspoon vanilla
Juice and rind of ½ orange
2¾ cups flour
2 teaspoons baking powder

¼ teaspoon (scant) salt
Suggestions for filling: Solo
  canned poppy filling
  (raisins can be added);
  mixture of jam and nuts;
  mixture of cooked prunes,
  honey, nuts, and raisins

Mix together eggs and sugar. Add oil, vanilla, orange juice, and rind. Sift together flour, baking powder, and salt. Add egg mixture. Roll to ¼ inch thick; cut into rounds with glass dipped in flour. Place spoonful of filling in center. Draw up three sides to center to form triangle. Pinch edges together. Brush tops with beaten egg. Bake on greased cookie sheet at 350°F about 20 minutes or until browned. Makes approximately 1½ dozen small haman taschen; 12 large haman taschen.

sour-cream-dough haman taschen

¼ pound butter
½ cup (scant) sugar
2 eggs

2 heaping cups flour
1½ teaspoons baking powder
Sour cream

Cream together butter and sugar. Add eggs; beat thoroughly.

Sift together flour and baking powder. Add to creamed mixture; mix well. Add enough sour cream to moisten dough to roll. Refrigerate a while if necessary. Roll out; cut into rounds. Fill; brush tops with beaten egg. Bake on greased cookie sheet at 350°F 20 minutes or until browned. Makes approximately 2½ dozen small or 1½ dozen large.

butter horns

This is my mother's recipe that she has had for years and years, and they are absolutely fantastic! Instead of butter, she uses vegetable shortening, so they will be parve.

1 small cake yeast
¼ cup warm water
2 tablespoons sugar
2 cups flour
Pinch of salt
1 cup vegetable shortening

2 egg yolks, well beaten
2 egg whites
½ cup sugar
Chopped nuts (walnuts or
    pecans)
Cinnamon and sugar mixture

Mix together yeast, water, and sugar in bowl; let stand.

Mix together flour and salt. Cut in shortening. Add egg yolks and yeast mixture; mix well. Knead dough until smooth. Let sit 1 hour.

Beat egg whites with sugar until peaks form.

Cut dough into 4 pieces. Roll each piece thin. Spread egg-white mixture on dough; sprinkle with nuts and cinnamon and sugar. Cut into 6 or 8 pieces; roll each piece. Form into crescent shapes. Place on greased cookie sheet. Bake at 350°F about 20 minutes or until lightly browned. Makes about 2½ dozen.

sour-cream horns

2 cups flour, sifted
½ pint sour cream
½ pound butter

nut filling

1 cup chopped nuts, 1 teaspoon cinnamon, and
2 tablespoons sugar mixed together
Confectioners' sugar

Sift flour.

Blend sour cream, butter, and flour together until dough forms. Let stand in refrigerator overnight.

Working with small amount of dough, roll out on floured surface into rectangle. Cut into triangles. Fill with nut filling or filling of your choice. Roll up each triangle; curve into crescent shape. Bake on cookie sheet at 375°F approximately 12 minutes or until lightly browned. When cool, sprinkle with confectioners' sugar. If freezing, sprinkle with confectioners' sugar before serving. Makes about 5 dozen.

50

angel-food cake

This cake is very good, especially with whipped cream.

1 cup sifted cake flour	**1¼ teaspoons cream of tartar**
1½ cups sugar	**1¼ teaspoons almond extract**
¼ teaspoon salt	**Toasted slivered almonds**
12 egg whites	**Confectioners' sugar**

Sift flour 4 times with ¾ cup sugar and salt.

Beat egg whites with cream of tartar until soft peaks form. Add remaining sugar, 2 tablespoons at a time, beating well after each addition. Sift ¼ cup flour mixture over egg whites; fold in carefully. Fold in remaining flour mixture by fourths. Slowly add almond extract; fold in well. Spoon into 10-inch tube pan. Bake in preheated 375°F oven 35 to 40 minutes or until cake tests done. Invert pan; cool completely. Remove from pan. Sprinkle almonds on top; sprinkle with confectioner' sugar. Makes about 16 pieces.

carrot cake

2 cups sifted all-purpose flour
2 teaspoons baking powder
1½ teaspoons baking soda
1 teaspoon salt
2 teaspoons cinnamon
1½ cups salad oil
2 cups sugar
4 eggs
2 cups grated carrots
1 small can crushed pineapple
1½ cups chopped walnuts
1 teaspoon vanilla extract
Confectioners' sugar

Sift flour, baking powder, soda, salt, and cinnamon together.

Combine oil and sugar in large mixing bowl; beat thoroughly with electric mixer. Add eggs 1 at a time, beating well after each addition.

Sift flour mixture into egg mixture; beat thoroughly. Stir in carrots, pineapple, walnuts, and vanilla extract. Spread batter evenly into well-greased and floured 9 × 13-inch pan or 2 loaf pans. Bake in preheated 350°F oven 1 hour or until cake tests done. Let cool in pan 10 minutes, then place on cake rack. Dust with sifted confectioners' sugar. Makes 12 to 15 servings.

carrot cake

mother's honey cake

mother's honey cake

1 pound honey
1 teaspoon baking soda
4 eggs
1 cup sugar
1 cup oil
4 cups flour
1 teaspoon baking powder
1 teaspoon cinnamon
1 teaspoon ground anise
¼ teaspoon ground ginger
Pinch of salt
Raisins (optional)
Almonds for top (optional)

Warm honey in saucepan on low heat. Add baking soda; stir until honey stirs easily. Remove from heat.

Beat eggs and sugar until well blended. Add honey mixture, oil, flour, baking powder, cinnamon, anise, ginger, salt, and raisins. Pour batter into greased 9 × 13-inch pan or 2 loaf pans. Sprinkle almonds on top. Bake at 325°F about 1 hour or until cake tests done.

If desired, almonds can also be folded into batter. Slices of cake can be spread with cream cheese, as in the picture, or with softened butter. Makes approximately 24 slices.

poppy cake

¼ pound plus 2 tablespoons
  butter
1 cup (scant) sugar
1 teaspoon vanilla extract
Pinch of salt
4 eggs
1⅔ cups flour

1 teaspoon baking powder
1 cup canned poppy-seed
  filling
⅓ cup ground almonds
½ teaspoon almond extract
½ ounce rum
Margarine

icing

¾ cup confectioners' sugar
3 tablespoons lemon juice
1 tablespoon hot water

In large bowl cream together butter, sugar, vanilla extract, and salt until
fluffy. Add eggs 1 at a time, mixing well after each addition. Gently
spoon flour and baking powder on top of mixture; fold in. Stir until
dough is smooth. Put one-third of dough aside in bowl. Add poppy-seed
filling, almonds, almond extract, and rum to remaining dough. Mix
together thoroughly.

Generously grease 7 × 11-inch pan with margarine. On bottom spread
layer of plain dough, then layer of dough mixed with poppy-seed filling.
Again spread layer of plain dough and another layer of poppy-seed
dough; top with remaining plain dough. Bake in preheated 350°F oven
about 40 to 45 minutes or until done. Remove cake from oven; turn
upside down on cake rack.

Mix together icing ingredients until smooth, adding more water if
necessary.

While cake is warm, cover with icing, letting it run down sides. Let cool;
cut into squres. Makes about 20 pieces.

honey cake

1 pint honey
1 cup sugar
8 eggs, separated
3 cups cake flour
½ teaspoon baking soda
2 teaspoons baking powder

1 teaspoon cinnamon
1 teaspoon allspice
1 teaspoon cocoa
1 cup strong black coffee
½ cup blanched slivered
  almonds

Cream honey and sugar 15 minutes. Add egg yolks; blend well.

Sift together dry ingredients. Add alternately with coffee. Fold in stiffly beaten egg whites. Bake in 2 square pans (put one cake in freezer) or large springform pan. Grease pans. Line pans with waxed paper; grease paper. Pour in batter; and sprinkle almonds on top. Bake at 350°F 45 to 55 minutes. Makes approximately 20 slices.

chanukah butter cookies

These cookies are delectable. My family looks forward to these from year to year.

½ pound butter
1 cup sugar
2 eggs
1 tablespoon cold water
1 teaspoon vanilla
1 teaspoon baking powder
3 cups flour
½ teaspoon (or less) salt

Cream butter. Add sugar; cream together. Add eggs, water, and vanilla.

Sift together baking powder, 1 cup flour, and salt. Add to creamed mixture; mix well. Add 2 cups flour; mix with wooden spoon. Refrigerate several hours or overnight. Roll out; cut into shapes with Chanukah cookie cutters. Bake at 400°F approximately 10 minutes or until browned.

These can be frosted with confectioners' sugar blended with enough milk to make it spreadable and vanilla to taste. Tint frosting a pale blue. Makes about 4 dozen, depending on size of cookie cutters.

meringue melt-aways

4 egg whites
2 cups sugar
3 tablespoons vinegar
1 teaspoon vanilla

Beat egg whites until very stiff. Beat in sugar gradually. Add vinegar and vanilla. Drop from teaspoon onto cookie sheet covered with brown paper. Bake at 325°F 20 minutes or until very lightly browned. Makes approximately 7 dozen.

passover ice-box cookies

¼ pound butter (or ½ cup oil)
1 cup sugar
2 eggs
1 cup cake meal
½ cup chopped nuts
Juice from ½ small lemon
Pinch of salt

Cream butter and sugar. Add rest of ingredients, mixing well. Form into 2 rolls. Wrap in waxed paper; refrigerate overnight. Slice. Bake on ungreased cookie sheet at 350°F about 15 minutes or until browned. Makes about 3 dozen cookies.

passover nut cookies

5 eggs
1½ cups cake meal
2 tablespoons potato starch
½ cup oil
1 cup sugar
1 cup ground nuts

Mix all ingredients together. Roll; shape into circles about size of half dollar. Bake at 400°F 10 minutes. Makes approximately 4 dozen.

poppy-seed cookies

3 eggs
1 cup sugar
¾ cup oil
Juice and rind of 1 orange
4 cups flour
2 teaspoons baking powder
½ teaspoon salt
¼ cup poppy seeds

Beat eggs. Add sugar, oil, orange juice, and rind. Add flour, baking powder, salt, and poppy seeds; mix thoroughly. Roll thin; cut into desired shapes. Bake on cookie sheet at 350°F approximately 8 to 10 minutes or until lightly browned. Makes about 5 dozen cookies, depending on size.

passover frosting

This is excellent with any kind of sponge cake.

1 egg white
Pinch of salt
1½ cups sugar
1 cup fresh strawberries, crushed

Beat egg white with salt. Gradually add sugar, beating until stiff. Fold in strawberries. Will frost 1 sponge cake.

lemon dessert mold

1 large package lemon gelatin
1½ cups boiling water
1 small can frozen lemonade,
   unthawed

1 carton (½ pint) Rich's
   Richwhip topping, whipped

Dissolve gelatin in boiling water. Immediately add lemonade; stir until completely thawed. Chill until gelatin just begins to congeal. Fold into whipped topping. Pour into mold or glass bowl; let set several hours or overnight. Makes 6 servings.

belle's trifle

This recipe was given to my mother-in-law years ago by an English friend. My mother-in-law gave the recipe to me, and I have been making it for years. It becomes an instant favorite of everyone who samples it. Even though it is not a traditional Jewish recipe, I wanted to share it with you, because it is so good and makes a delightful dessert.

In place of ladyfingers you can substitute store-bought jelly roll cut into thin slices. This works very well and is a good time-saver.

Ladyfingers, halved (number
   depends on size of bowl)
Rasberry jam, preferably
   seedless
Clear glass bowl
3-ounce box raspberry gelatin
1 cup boiling water

½ cup sherry
1 3¼-ounce box vanilla
   pudding
1½ pints whipping cream
Sugar to taste
Vanilla

Spread each half of ladyfingers with raspberry jam; put back together sandwich-style. Line bottom and halfway up sides of glass bowl with ladyfingers.

Prepare gelatin by dissolving in boiling water. Add sherry; let cool slightly. Pour over ladyfingers; let set.

Prepare vanilla pudding according to package directions. Carefully pour pudding into bowl to make another layer. Cover with cream whipped with sugar to taste and vanilla. Makes 6 servings.

parve ice cream

1 container kosher parve
   dessert whip
1 8-ounce jar marshmallow
   fluff

1 pint mashed fresh
   strawberries (or frozen
   strawberries or raspberries,
   or fruit of your choice)

Whip dessert whip until stiff. Blend in marshmallow fluff. Add fruit; mix thoroughly. Freeze in large bowl (looks pretty in glass bowl) or in individual parfait glasses. Makes 8 servings.

taiglach

To serve on a sweet table, taiglach can be put into small paper cupcake cups.

¼ cup vegetable oil
4 eggs
2¼ cups flour
1 teaspoon baking powder
1 pound honey
2 teaspoons ginger
⅛ teaspoon cinnamon
½ pound brown sugar
1 cup walnuts
¼ cup raisins

Mix oil and eggs well. Add flour and baking powder. Knead with hands. Dough should be firm but not too hard. Break off piece; roll with hands to make rope about ½ inch thick. Cut into pieces about ½ inch long. Place pieces on cookie sheet. Bake in 350°F oven about 15 minutes or until lightly browned.

Meanwhile put honey, ginger, cinnamon, and brown sugar in large pot. Bring to boil quickly. Drop baked taiglach into mixture. Stir constantly with wooden spoon. When taiglach turn reddish brown, drop in nuts and raisins. Cook, stirring, 30 minutes. Pour into large, well-greased pan; cut when hard. Makes about 6 dozen.

dairy strudel dough

¼ pound margarine, softened
¼ pound butter, softened
½ pint sour cream
2 cups flour
Filling of your choice
Cinnamon and sugar

Mix ingredients together. Divide into 5 balls. Refrigerate at least 6 hours. Roll out each ball, 1 at a time. Spread with your favorite preserves or a mixture of several different kinds, then with raisins and nuts, then cinnamon and sugar, and, if desired, coconut. Roll up each part carefully. Before baking, sprinkle each with cinnamon and sugar. Bake in 375°F oven 45 minutes or until nicely browned. Let cool before cutting into diagonal slices approximately 1 inch thick. Makes about 3½ dozen pieces.

easy strudel

½ pound butter, softened
½ pint sour cream
2 cups flour
Peach or orange marmalade
Maraschino cherries, cut into small pieces
Pecans, chopped fine

Thoroughly mix together butter, sour cream, and flour. Form into ball; refrigerate 1 hour. Cut into 4 portions; roll each portion into thin rectangular shape. Spread with choice of marmalade or mixture of both; sprinkle with cherries and pecans. Roll jelly-roll fashion; place on lightly greased cookie sheet. Make slight cuts as guide for slicing when taken out of oven. Bake in 375°F oven 30 minutes. Makes about 50 slices.

apple strudel

strudel dough

2 cups flour
1 tablespoon sugar
Pinch of salt
1 egg

3 tablespoons melted
shortening (or oil)
1 cup (approximately) cold
water

Sift dry ingredients into mixing bowl; make well in center. Add egg and melted shortening. Stir to combine. Add a little water at a time to make dough firm enough to handle. Toss onto lightly floured board; knead 4 minutes. Roll out very thin.

apple filling

3 cups thinly sliced apples
¾ cup sugar
½ teaspoon cinnamon
Dash of nutmeg
Raisins (optional)

4 tablespoons melted shortening
Confectioners' sugar

Mix apples with sugar, cinnamon, nutmeg, and raisins.

Place row of apple mixture on edge of dough. Roll jelly-roll fashion very carefully, tucking in ends. Place on well-greased cookie sheet. Brush tops with melted shortening. Bake in 375°F oven 45 minutes or until nicely browned. Sprinkle with sifted confectioners' sugar. Makes approximately 15 slices.

apple strudel

fried puffy twists

These are very easy to prepare and very delicious!

2 eggs
1 teaspoon baking powder
Pinch of salt
3 tablespoons sugar
1 tablespoon vinegar
¼ cup oil
3 tablespoons warm water
1 cup flour, sifted (maybe more)
Oil for frying
Confectioners' sugar

Beat eggs. Add baking powder, salt, sugar, vinegar, oil, and water; blend well. Add flour; mix well to make dough. Toss on floured board, adding more flour if necessary until dough is workable. Cut off small pieces; roll into thin rectangular shapes. If desired, as in picture, cut lengthwise slit through center of rectangular strip of dough and pull one end through, making a twist. Fry quickly in hot oil in skillet or deep fryer until browned. Drain on paper toweling. Sprinkle with sifted confectioners' sugar and enjoy! Makes about 5 to 6 dozen.

fried puffy twists

miscellaneous

busy-day blintzes

1 loaf thin-sliced white sandwich bread	Sugar to taste
8 ounces cream cheese	Melted butter

Cut crusts off bread slices. Roll each slice with rolling pin to make rectangle.

Mix cream cheese with sugar. Spread on each slice of bread; roll jelly-roll fashion. Cut each roll in half.

Melt butter; dip each roll into melted butter, then place on cookie sheet. Bake at 325°F until lightly browned. Makes approximately 3 dozen.

cheese blintzes

blintz batter

4 eggs	1 cup milk
1 teaspoon salt	Oil for frying
1 cup flour	

Beat eggs and salt. Add flour alternately with milk.

Heat oil in frying pan. Pour only enough batter into pan to make very thin pancake, tipping pan to let batter completely cover pan. Fry on one side until it bubbles. Turn pan over; let pancake fall out onto waxed paper.

cheese filling

1½ pounds dry cottage cheese	Sugar to taste
2 egg yolks	Cinnamon to taste

Combine filling ingredients.

Place 1 tablespoon filling mixture on browned side of each pancake. Fold in sides to form square; roll. Brown in frying pan.

Serve blintzes hot, accompanied by sour cream. Makes about 20 blintzes.

passover cheese blintzes

blintz batter

¾ cup matzo cake flour
1½ cups water
3 eggs, beaten
½ teaspoon salt
Oil or butter for frying

Add flour and water alternately to eggs. Add salt. Batter will be thin. Pour small amount batter into 6- or 7-inch skillet or on griddle, spreading batter as thin as possible. Fry until brown; turn out on towel, browned-side-up.

cheese filling

1 pound cottage cheese
1 tablespoon cream
1 egg, beaten
¼ teaspoon salt
½ teaspoon sugar

Mix together filling ingredients.

Place small amount on one edge of blintze skin. Tuck in ends; roll up. Brown in butter. Serve with sour cream or sprinkle with sugar and cinnamon. Makes about 15 blintzes.

homemade horseradish (chraine)

1 pound horseradish root, peeled, grated
½ pound beets, peeled, grated
1 teaspoon salt
1 teaspoon sugar
¼ cup lemon juice

Mix everything together thoroughly. Store in refrigerator in covered glass jar.

rendering chicken fat (schmaltz)

Cut fatty skin and other fat particles into small pieces. Cover with cold water; cook in pot, uncovered, until water is almost evaporated. Reduce heat. Add diced onions; be generous. When onion pieces are brown, fat is done. When cool, remove onion pieces; use them in mashed potatoes, chopped liver, or stuffing. Store fat in covered jars. Can be frozen or kept in refrigerator.

index